MY FIRST 1001 WORDS

READ, LOOK & LEARN

PhP

PETER HADDOCK PUBLISHING

Plug and Chain

Plughole

Bath

Toilet

Toilet Paper

Tap

Wash Basin

3

Beach Towel

Cool Box

Seaweed

Shells

Cuttlefish

Pebbles

Starfish

Sun Hat

Back Brush

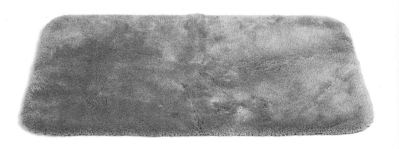

Bathmat

Soap Tray

Toy Boat

Rubber Duck

Sponge

Nail Brush

Soap

Eggcup

Cereal

Milk

Muesli

Tea

Jam

Toast

Orange Juice

9

Bucket

Cloth

Long-term
beauty treatment
for all paint types
including metallics

325 ml℮

Polish

Detergent

Rag

Car Sponge

Soapy Water

Squeegee

Bleach

Dustpan and Brush

Duster

Spray

Cleaner

Scrubbing Brush

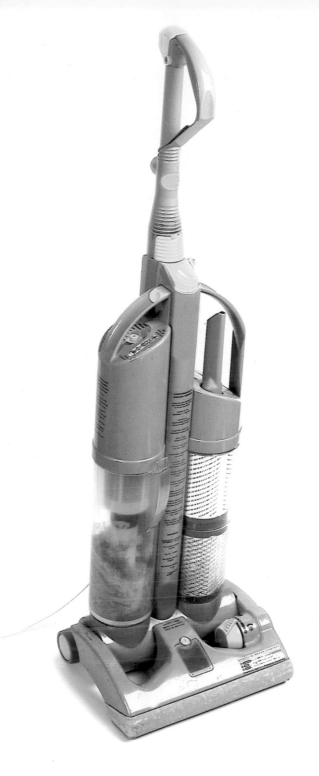

Vacuum Cleaner

13

Black

Blue

Red

White

Green

Grey

Yellow

Orange

15

Brown

Burgundy

Pink

Purple

Light Blue

Ochre

Turquoise

Lemon

17

Stile

Stream

Compass

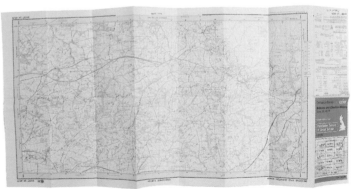

Map

Path

Daisy

Boots and Laces

Rain Hat

19

Drink

Cutlery

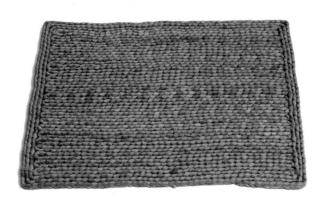

Place Mat

Loaf

Glass

Olives

Scrambled Eggs

Cork

KITCHEN

Fridge and Freezer

Cooker

Kettle

Microwave

Sink

Stool

Toaster

Wok

Hoe

Extension Lead

Wheelbarrow

Hose and Nozzle

Wire

Lawnmower

Watering-can

Garden Tap

Boxer Shorts

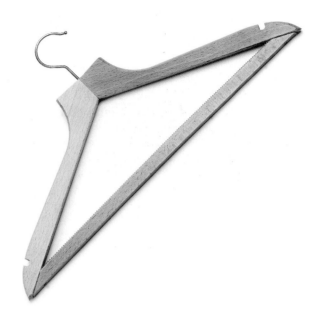

Coat Hanger

Trousers

Sweatshirt

Jumper and Sleeves

Socks

T-Shirt

Shirt and Collar

27

Field

Bark

Nettles

Twigs

Flowers   Sky

Tree   Bush

Banknotes

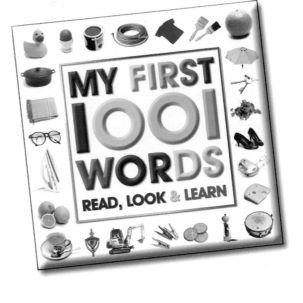

Book

Film

Magazine

Camera and Camera Case

Coins

Penknife

Sunglasses

Calculator

Document Case

Passport

Instructions

Notepad

Boxfile

Stapler

Staples

33

Paint Brushes

Decorator

Scraper

Spirit-level

Paint Roller

Paint

Step-ladder

Wallpaper

Bib

Peppermill

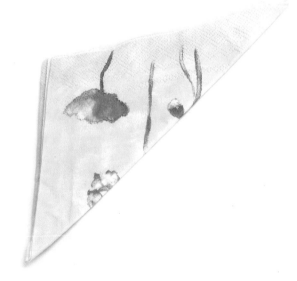

Serviette

Spoon

Sauce

Salt-Cellar

Fork

Knife

Bellows

Coal

Grate

Poker

Fire

Fireplace

Logs

Fire Tongs

Doorbell

Pane

Door Chain

Doormat

Plaque

Keyhole

Letterbox

Door Knocker

Padlock

Ladder

Cable

Nails

Digger & Driver

Bricks

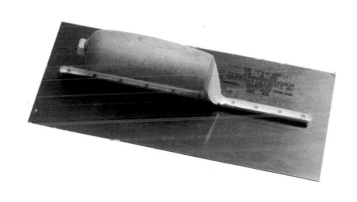

Float

Wire Wool

43

Bouncy Slide

Bouncy Castle

Spinner

Roundabout

Ferris Wheel   Helter-skelter

Trampoline   Waltzer

45

Mango

Pineapple

Peaches

Strawberry

Clementine

Melon

Pear and Stalk

Lemons

Apple

Dried Apricots

Lime

Blackberries

Banana

Kiwi Fruit

Cherries

Grapes

Birdbath

Patio

Bird Feeder

Pillar

Greenhouse

Garden

Sundial

Birdseed

51

Hedge

Fence

Pruning Saw

Flower Pot

Leaves   Grass

Seed Tray and Seedlings

GARDEN TOOLS

Broom

Garden Fork

Shears

Spade

Rake

Secateurs

Hand Fork

Trowel

Chutney

Eggs

Parsley

Juice

Jar

Carton

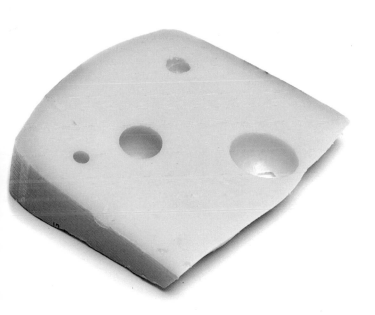

Cheese

Yoghurt

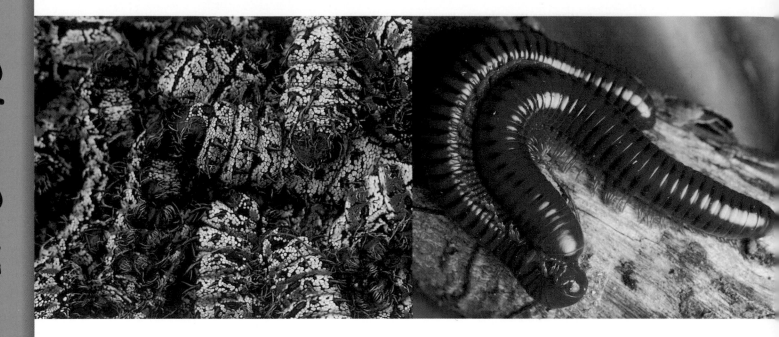

Caterpillars   Centipedes

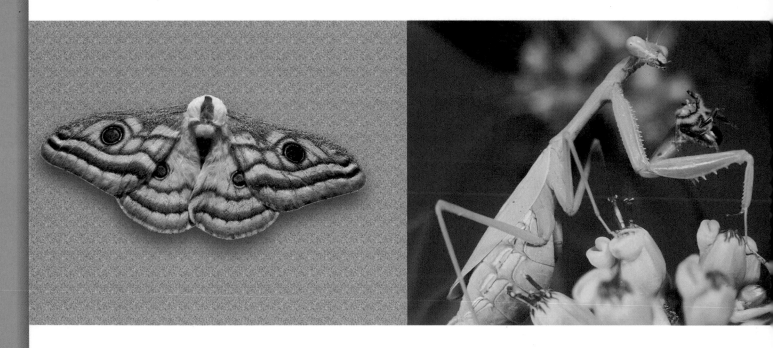

Moth   Praying Mantis

Snail

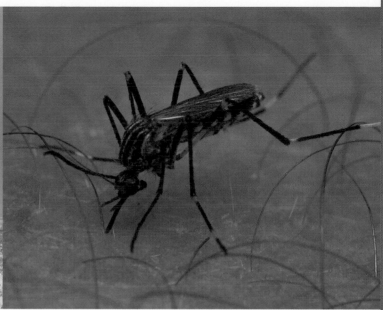

Mosquito

Scorpion

Fly

59

SOME JUNGLE ANIMALS

Cheetah

Beetle

Chimpanzee

Lion

Giraffes   Rhinoceros

Elephant   Tiger

Cat Food

Instant Coffee

Straws

Tea Bag

Match Box
and Matches

Spaghetti

pick the best
Red Kidney Beans
in water, sugar, salt added

Tin

Butter

Apron

Corkscrew

Strainer

Peeler

Tin-opener

Funnel

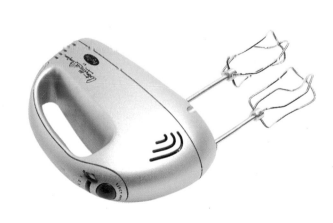

Mixer and Beaters

Scoop

Bread Knife and
Bread Board

Scales

Rolling pin

Saucepan

Frying-pan

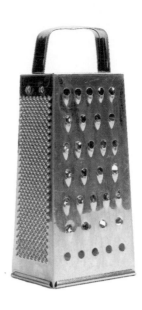

Grater

Sieve

Thermos

Casserole dish

Colander

Ladle

Lemon Squeezer

Fridge Magnets

Jug

Pasta

Pyrex Bowl

Fabric Conditioner

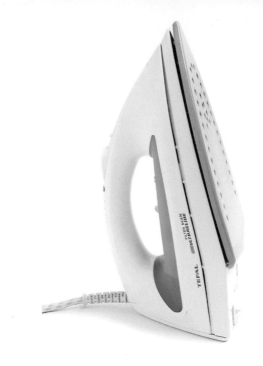

Iron

Pegs

Basket and Laundry

Ironing Board

Washing Liquid

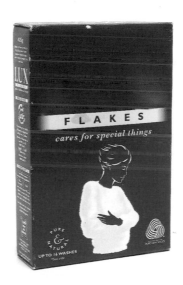

Washing Powder

71

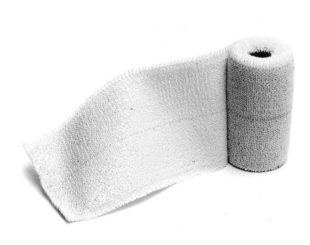

Bandage

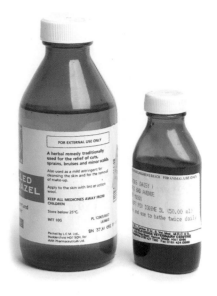

Medicine

Thermometer

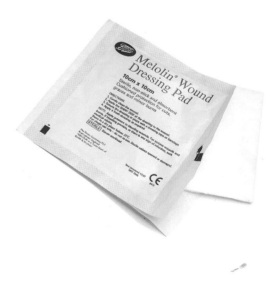

Dressing

Ointment

Plaster

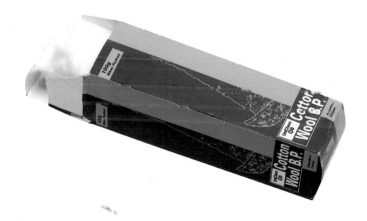

Cotton Wool

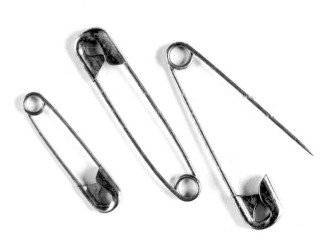

Safety Pins

Blouse

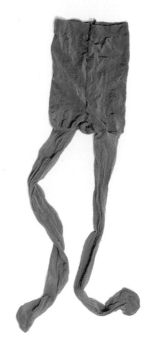

Tights

Skirt

High-heeled Shoes

Slippers

Nail file

Dress

Mules

Make-up Bag

Hair Dryer

Bag

Hand Cream

Hand cream

Mirror

Ring

Perfume

Tissues

Bracelet

Glasses

Lipstick

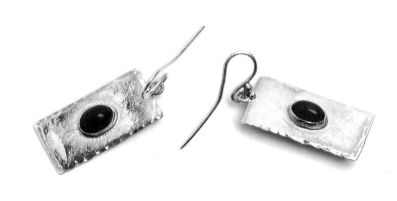

Earrings

Lotion

Hair Brush

Jewellery Box

Necklace

Frog

Fish

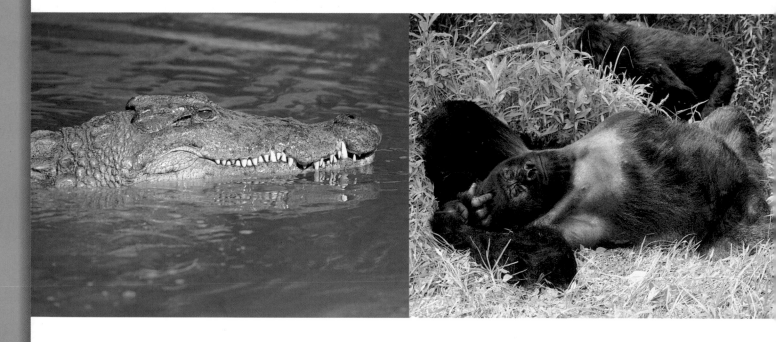

Alligator

Gorilla

Lizard

Turtle

Peacock

Snake

Anti-perspirant

Toothbrush

Razor

Shaving-brush

Flannel

Floss

Toothpaste

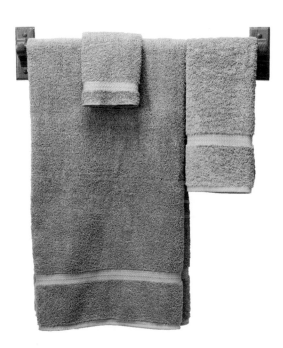

Towels and Towel Rail

83

Biscuits

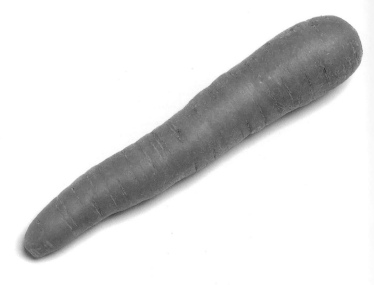

Carrot

Spring Onions

Rice

Salad

Parsnip

Peas and Peapods

Lentils

Feather

Net

Sunshade

Rope

Sunscreen

Picnic Hamper

Water Bottle

Sand

Briefcase

Fountain Pen

Wallet

Mobile Phone

Watch and Strap

Ink

Credit Card

House Keys

Clarinet

Drum

Synthesiser

Trombone

Trumpet

Recorder

Electric Guitar

Classical Guitar

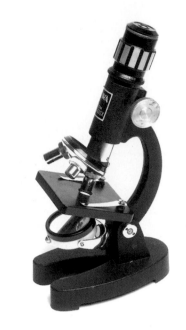

Microscope

Curtain & Rail

Mug

Computer

Mouse

Blanket

Money box

Dog & Dog bed

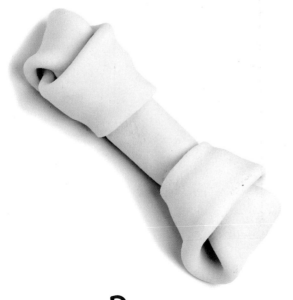

Bone

Dog bowl

Dog Biscuits

Dog brush

Dog Collar

Lead

NATURE

Beach & Shore   Cliffs

Waterfall   Woods

Desert & Dunes

Lake

Mountains

Countryside

Hole Punch

Keyboard

Tape and Dispenser

Paperclips

Rubber Bands

Cash Bag

Monitor

Pencil Sharpener

Clip

Marker Pen and Lid

Radio

Sticky Tack

Printer   Swivel Chair and Castors

Stamps   Coloured Pencils

Button

Cotton Reel

Needle

Ribbon

Knitting Needles

Wool

Thimble

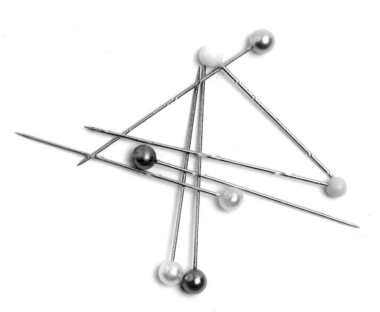

Pins

Arm Chair

Candle and Candlestick

Pot Plant

Picture and Frame

Clock

Table Lamp

Chair

Cushion

Compact Disc

Video Recorder

Loudspeaker

Remote Control

Television and Screen

Headphones

Video Cassette

Hi-Fi

Cricket Ball

Cricket Gloves

Cricket Pads

Bails

Cricket Bat

Stumps

Football

Tennis Racket

Table Tennis Ball

Squash Racket

Tennis Balls

Table Tennis Bat

Squash Ball

Golf Ball

THE STREET

Lamp post

Road Signs

Kerb and Gutter

Yellow Line

Wheelie Bin

Telegraph Pole

113

Bricklayer's Trowel

Drill Bits

Wire Brush

Bolt and Nut

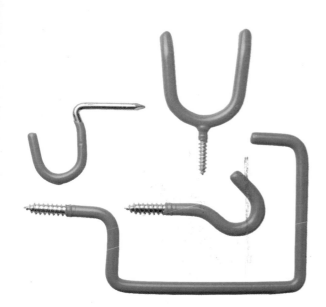

Hooks

Putty Knife

Crowbar

Set Square

Drill

Hammer

Cutters

Screwdriver

Spanner

Metal File

Panel Saw

Wood Plane

Chisel

Clamp

Hacksaw and Blade

Pliers

Tape Measure

Toolbox

Mallet

Teddy Bear

Toy Lorry

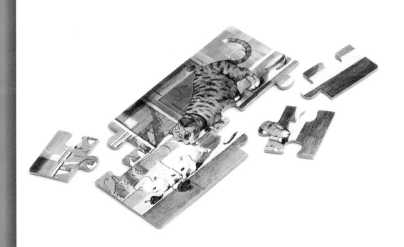

Jigsaw Puzzle

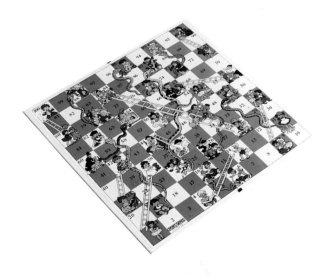

Snakes and Ladders

Model Train

Mascot

Toy Fire Engine

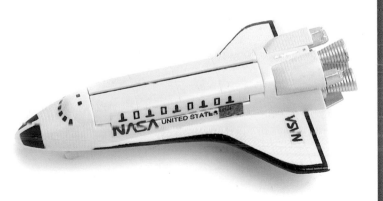

Space Shuttle

Coach

Dumper Truck

Boat

Tank

Steam Train

Lorry

Tow-Truck

Carriages

Aubergine

Red Pepper

Garlic and Clove

Mushroom

Cauliflower

Onion

Avacado and Stone

Broccoli

125

Plate

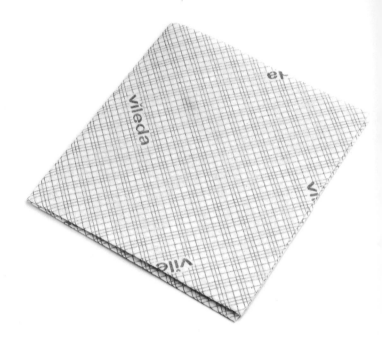

Dish Cloth

Scourer

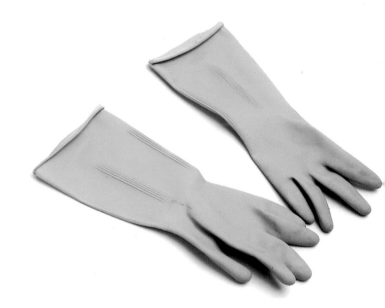

Rubber Gloves

Soapsuds

Tea Towel

Washing-up Liquid

Washing-up Brush

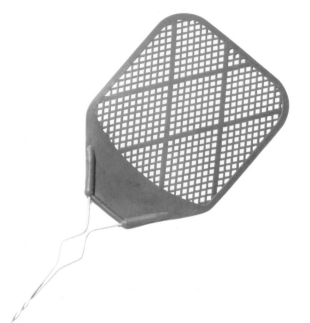

Fly Swat

Mat

Light Bulb

Oil Lamp

String

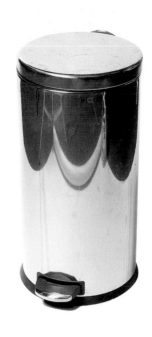

Waste Bin

Screws

Tube of Polish

129

WEATHER

Cloud

Lightning

Flood

Tornado

Rainbow

Snow

Sunset

Storm

Tomato Truss

Window Box and Polyanthus

Succulent

Sloes

Woodland

Jungle

Dressing Gown

Duvet

Sheet

Duvet Cover

Pillow

Stopper

Pillowcase

Hot Water Bottle

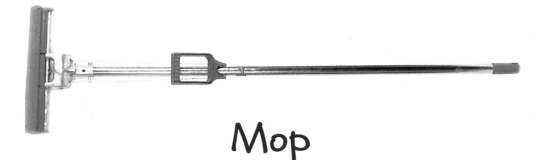

Sweeping Brush

Mop

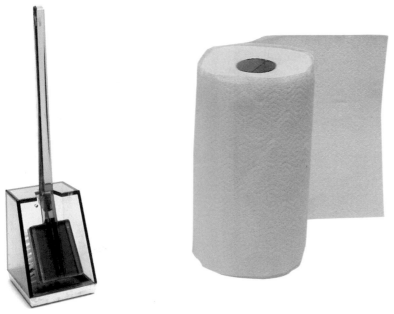

BALL POINT PEN
STAIN REMOVER

REMOVES BALL POINT PEN
STAINS FROM FABRICS
ALSO STRONGLY COLOURED
STAINS SUCH AS KETCHUP
AND TYPEWRITER RIBBON
50 ml ℮

Toilet
Brush

Kitchen
Paper

Stain
Remover

Wet Wipes

Wax
Polish

Carpet
Shampooer

Cap and Peak

Corduroy Shirt

Fleece

Scarf

Woolly Gloves

Tie

Suit Jacket

Jeans and Belt

Anorak

Umbrella

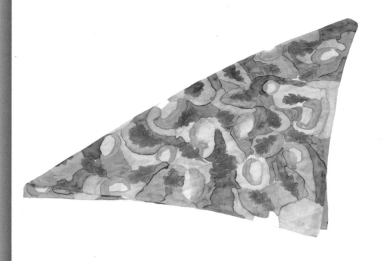

Headscarf

Puddle

Raindrops

Pac-a-Mac

Wellingtons

Rain

141

Carpet

Lino

Tarmac

Parquet

Rug

Floorboards

Concrete

Earth

143

Bass Guitar

Tambourine

Piano

Microphone

Piano Stool

Sheet Music

Musical Notes

Music-Stand

145

Building Blocks

Board Game

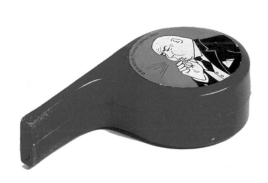

Whistle

Colouring Book

Dice

Railway Track

Toy Trunk

Globe

147

Cling Film

Sandwich Box

Ham Roll

Sweets

Tomato

Sandwich

Crisps

Foil

Wax Crayons

Rubber

Drawings

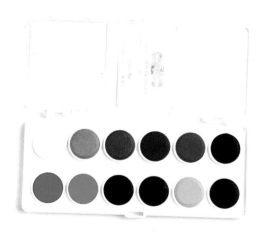

Water Colours
and Paint box

Poster Paints

Tubes

Felt Tip Pens

Flip-flops

Kit Bag

Swimming Cap

Swimsuit

Goggles

Water-wings

Swimming trunks

Joggers

Jump Leads

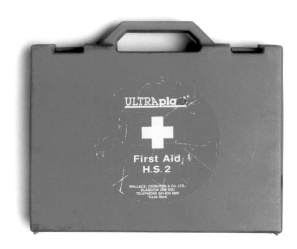

First Aid Kit

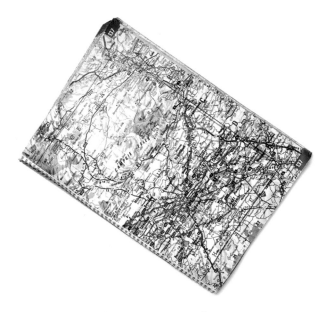

Road Atlas

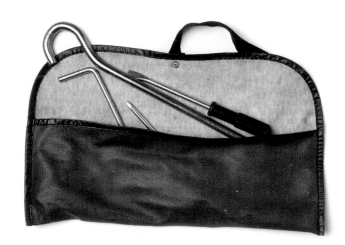

Toolkit

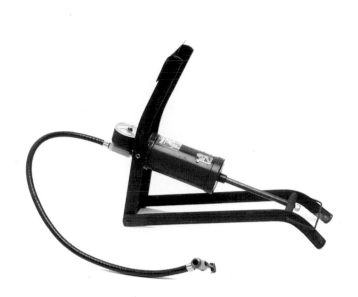

Foot Pump

Wheel-nut Spanner

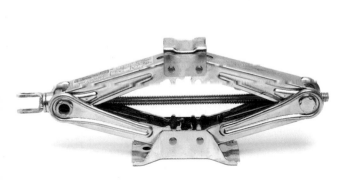

Car Jack

Engine Oil

Masking Tape

Oil

Putty Knife

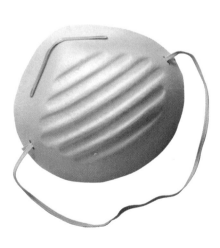

Face mask

Sandpaper

Scissors

Safety Goggles

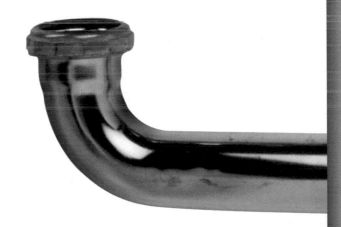

Pipe

Coffee Beans

Fried Egg

Mustard

Pine Nut Kernels

Ginger Root

Kidney Beans

Tub

Watercress

Toy Aeroplane

Blind

Flash Cards

Playdough

Toy Chest

Fan

Playing Cards

Rocket

Card

Soft Toy

Lollipops

Mobile

Puppet

Tricycle

Pushchair

Present

163

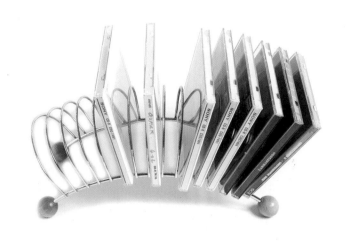

CD Rack

Toy Motor Bike

Toy Train

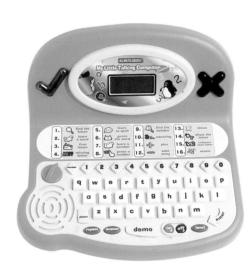

Toy Typewriter

Tiddlywinks

Robot

Pullover

Binoculars

165

Exercise Book

Packed Lunch

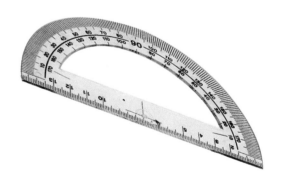

Protractor

Ruler

Satchel

Pencil-case

Folder

Drinking Bottle

Barometer

Book Shelves

Painting

Goblet

Cat's Bed

Coffee Table

Cup & Saucer

Light

BIRDS

Eagle

Owl

Kingfisher

Pelicans

Parrot

Seagull

Vulture

Waders

Drain

Manhole Cover

Garage

Signpost

Satellite Dish   Paving-stone

Telephone Box   Parking Bay

Change

Letter and Envelope

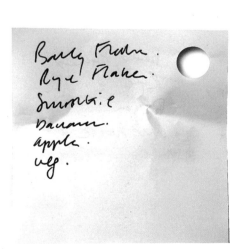

Shopping List

Purse

Car Keys and Key-fob

Receipt

Address Book

Telephone Directory

175

Garden Gate   Litter Bin   Fungus

Duck   Dove

IN LOVING MEMORY OF MY DEAR HUSBAND KENNETH WEAIRE 1922-1993
DEARLY LOVED, SADLY MISSED, REMEMBERED ALWAYS BY FAMILY AND FRIENDS

Park Bench

Statue   Icicles

Almonds

Chocolate Biscuits

Ice Cream Cone

Hazelnuts

Brazil Nuts

Chocolate Bar and Wrapper

Fondants

Peanuts

Badminton Racket

Cycle Helmet

Shuttlecock

Skateboard

Holdall

Trainers

Tennis Shorts

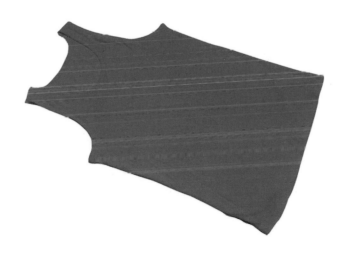

Vest

WILD ANIMALS

Antelope

Hippopotamus

Flamingo

Dolphin

Deer

Monkey

Lemur

Tortoise

Flower

Bud

Bloom

Stem

Stalk

Vein

Leaf

Plant

Gerbera

Lily

Rose

Poppy

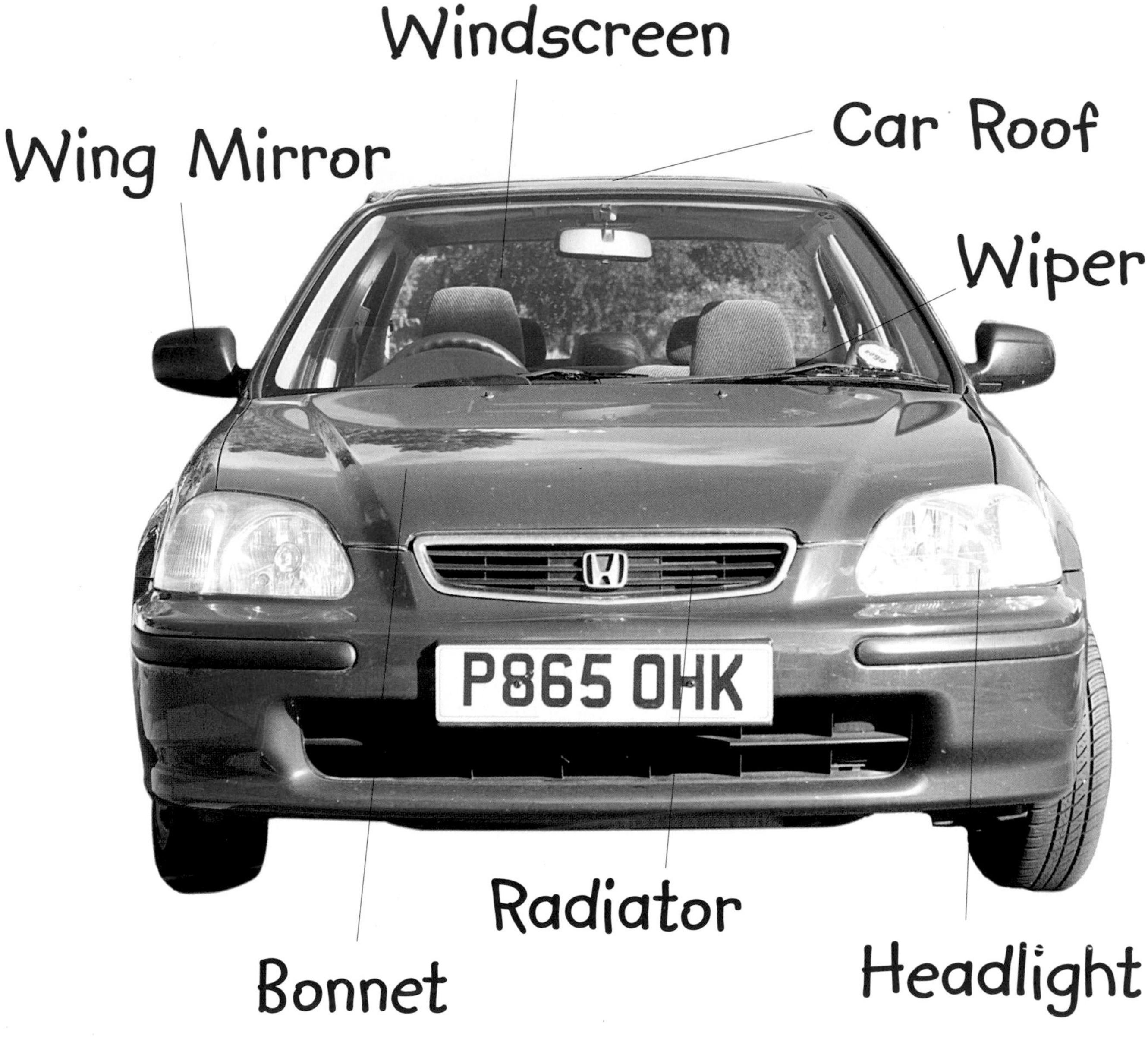

Windscreen

Car Roof

Wing Mirror

Wiper

P865 OHK

Radiator

Bonnet

Headlight

Front

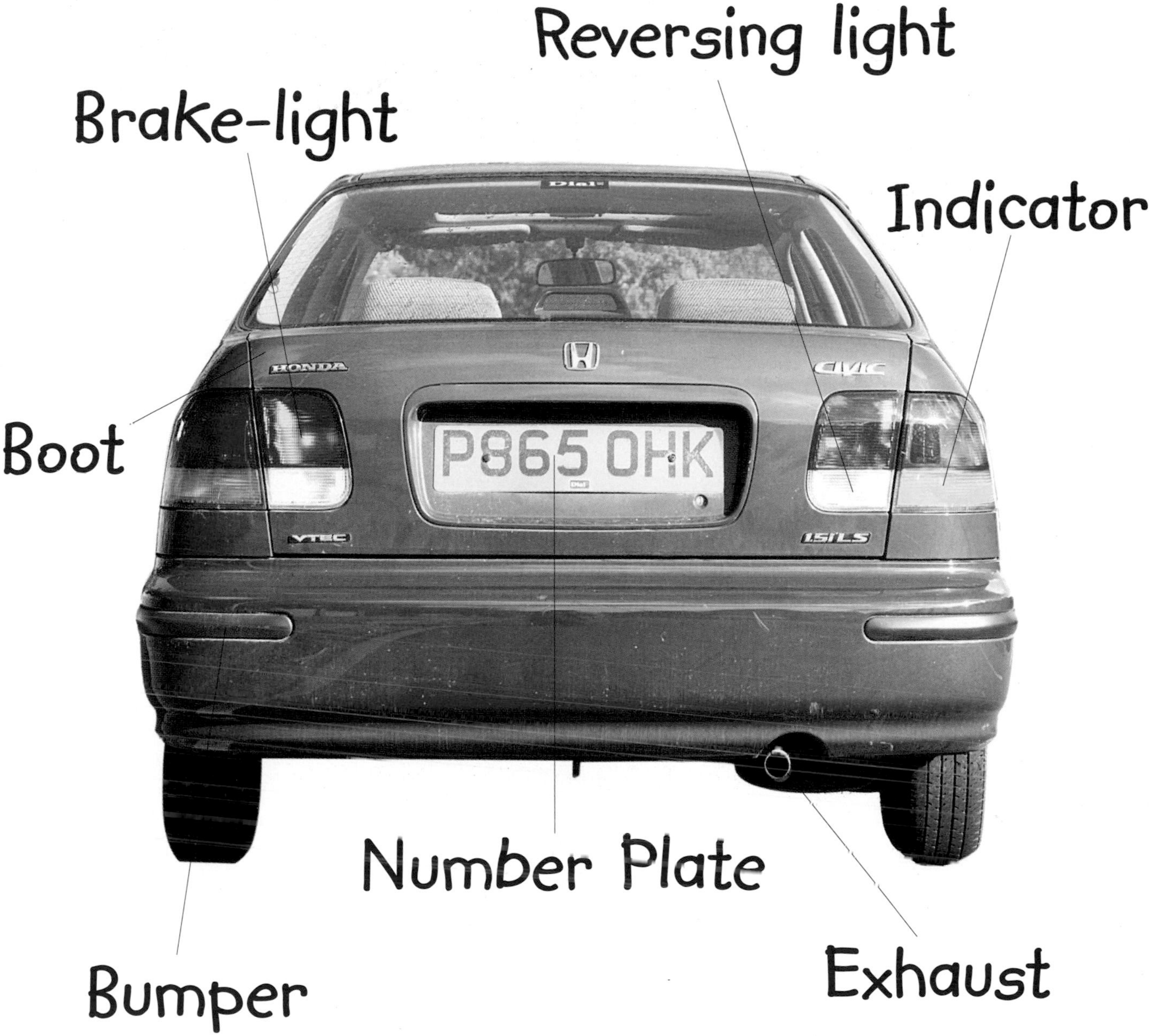
Reversing light
Brake-light
Indicator
Boot
P865 OHK
HONDA
CIVIC
VTEC
Number Plate
Bumper
Exhaust

Back

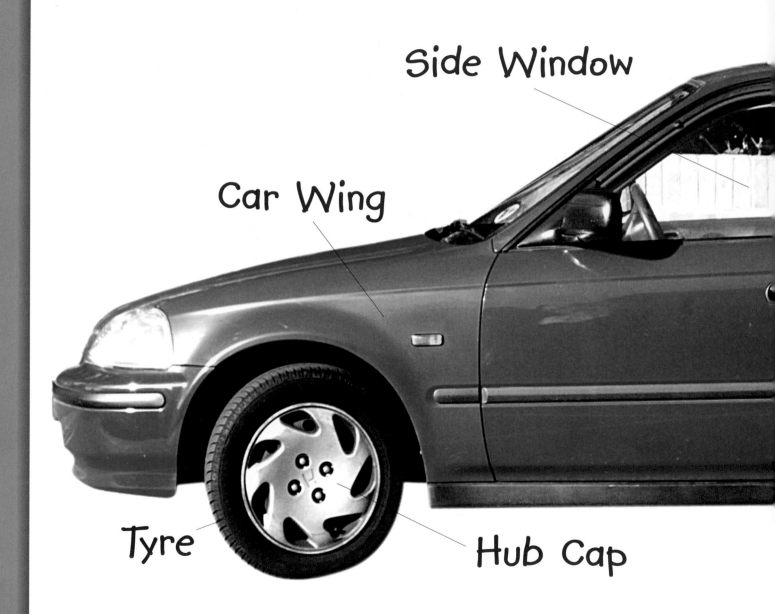

Side Window

Car Wing

Tyre

Hub Cap

Side

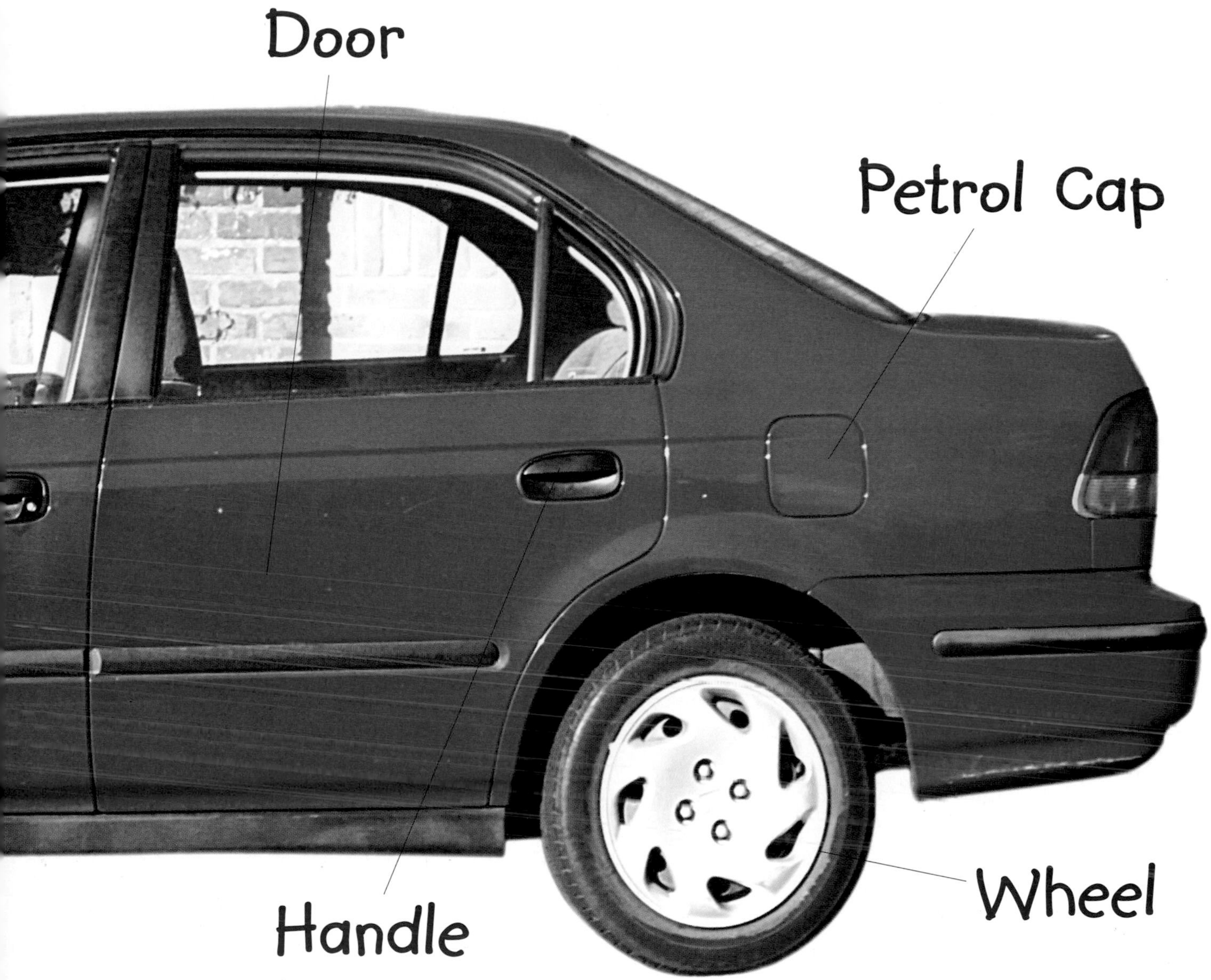

Door

Petrol Cap

Handle

Wheel

Roof

Gable

Bay

Driveway

Wall

Chimney

Window

Porch

Front Door

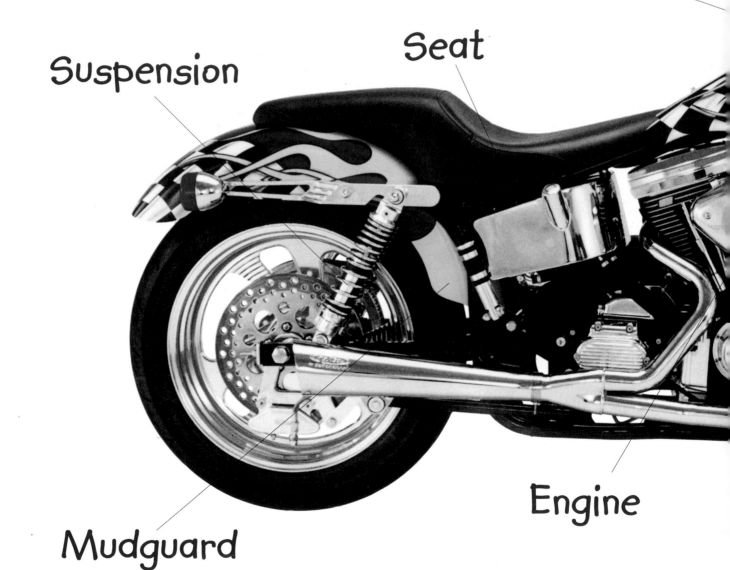

Petrol Tank

Seat

Suspension

Mudguard

Engine

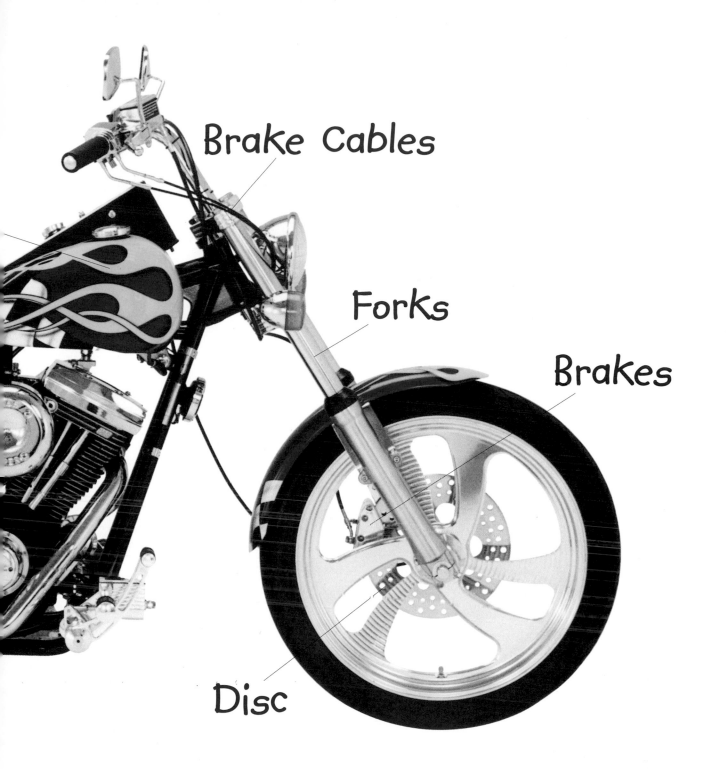

Brake Cables

Forks

Brakes

Disc

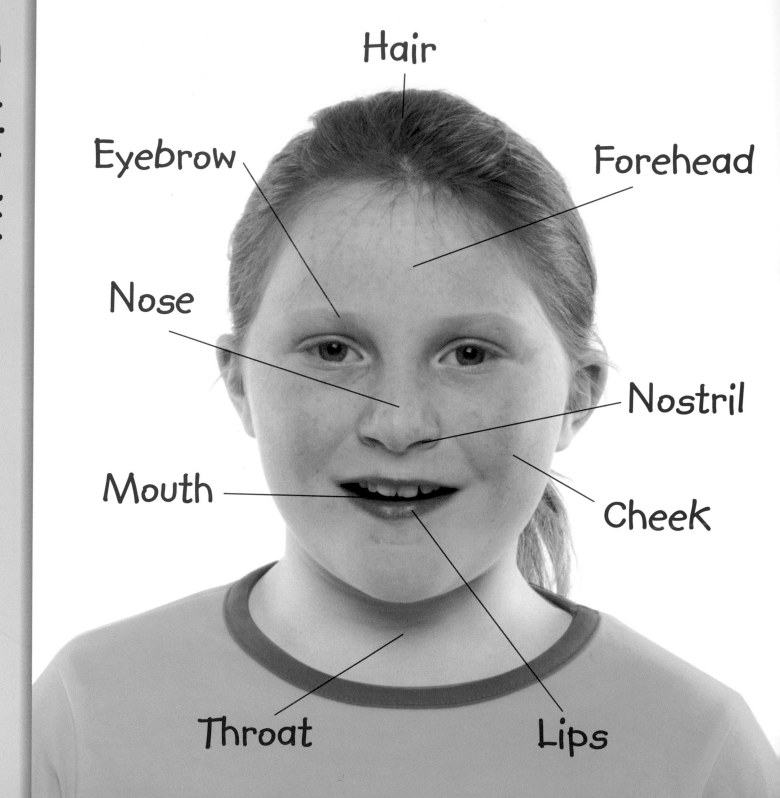

Hair

Eyebrow

Forehead

Nose

Nostril

Mouth

Cheek

Throat

Lips

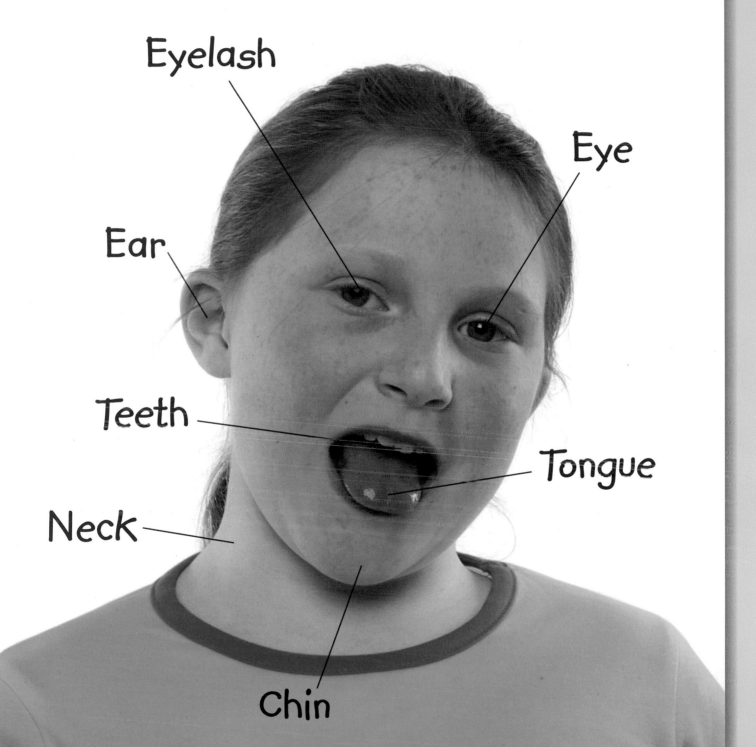

Eyelash

Eye

Ear

Teeth

Tongue

Neck

Chin

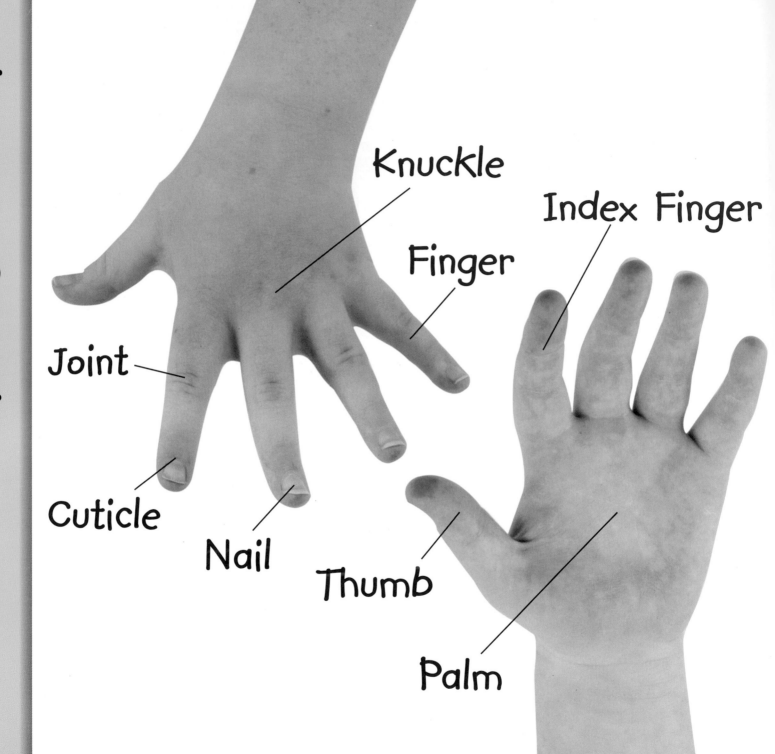

Knuckle

Index Finger

Finger

Joint

Cuticle

Nail

Thumb

Palm

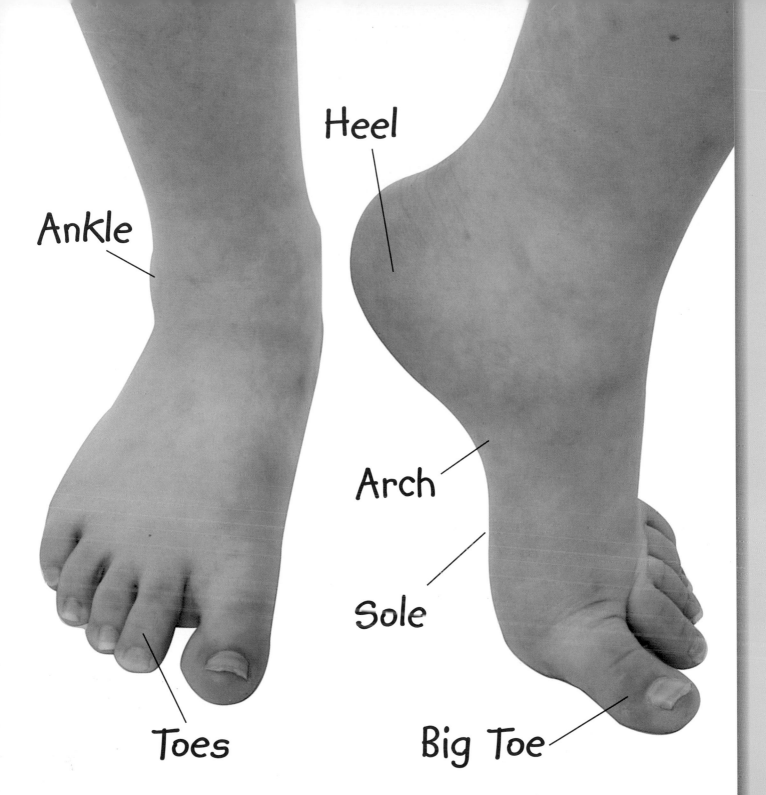

Heel

Ankle

Arch

Sole

Toes

Big Toe

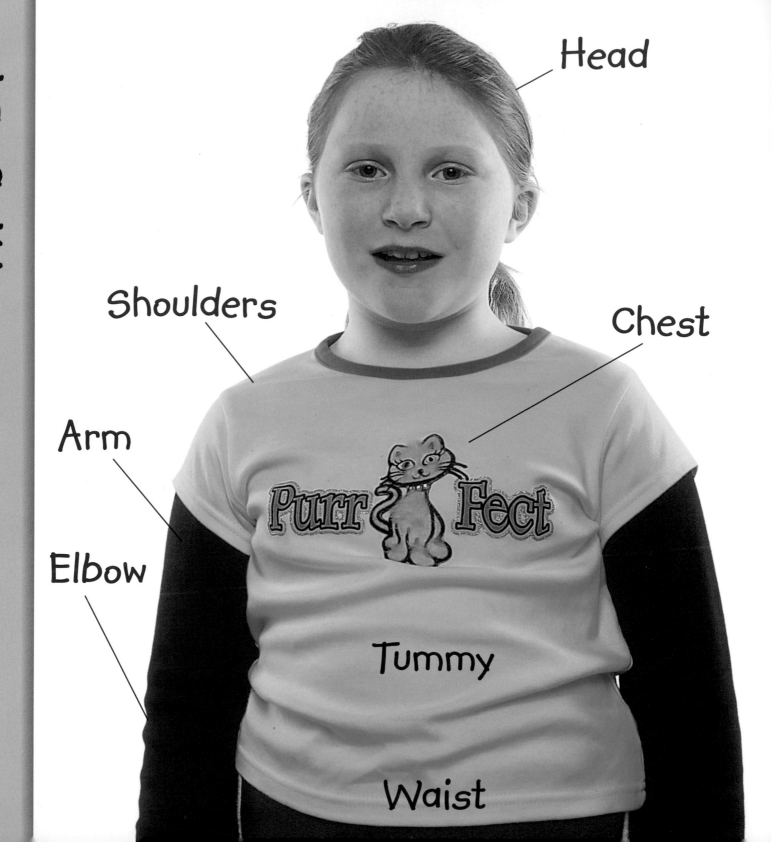

Head

Shoulders

Chest

Arm

Elbow

Tummy

Waist

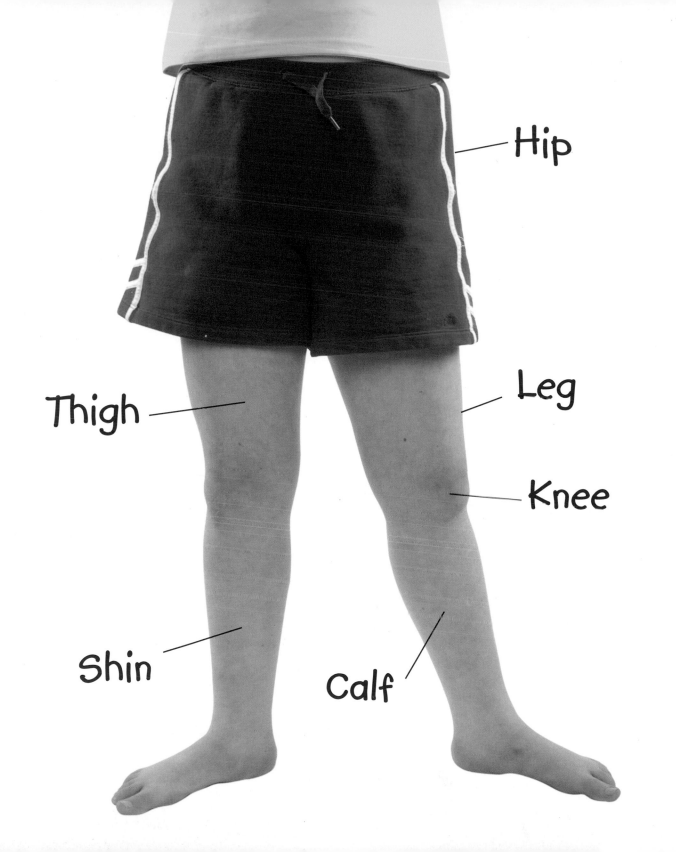

Hip

Thigh

Leg

Knee

Shin

Calf

Bull

Rabbit

Sheep

Hen

Goat

Ram

Horses

Goose

Bollard

Bottle Banks

Pelican Crossing   **Bus Shelter**

Public Toilet

Parking Meter

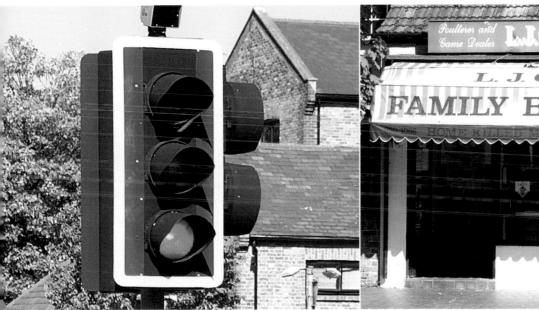

Traffic Lights

Butcher's Shop

Car Showroom

Fish and Chip Shop

Public House

Warehouse

Flats

Car Garage

Scaffolding

Railing

Pylon

City

Suspension Bridge

Trolley Park

TV Mast

Barrier

Flag & Flag Pole

Rushes

Aviary

Willow Tree

Island

Copse

Obelisk

Fir Tree

Fountain

Zero

One

Four

Five

Two

Three

Six

Seven

Hot Air Balloon

Emu

Skyscrapers

Wind Farm

Hang-glider

Oil-rig

Barn

Radar Dish

Swing

Beam

Bouncer

Climbing Frame

See-saw

Slide

Rollerblading

Cycling

215

Pen

Berries

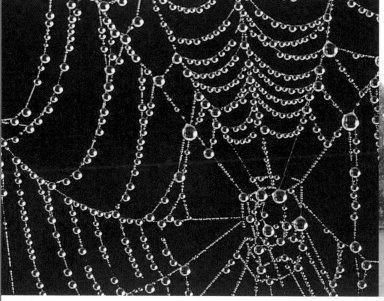

Spider's Web

Lake

Canada Goose

Flock

Swan

Palm Tree

217

Eight

Nine

Twelve

Thirteen

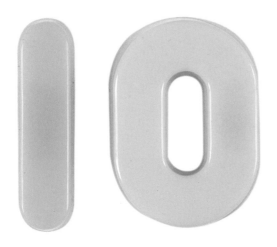

Ten

Eleven

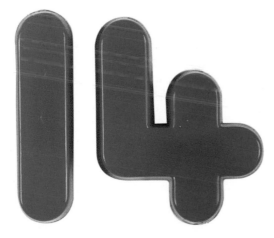

Fourteen

Fifteen

Sixteen

Seventeen

Twenty

Thirty

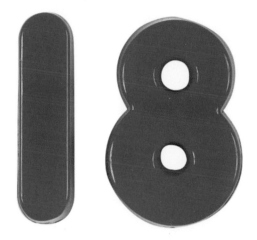

Eighteen

Nineteen

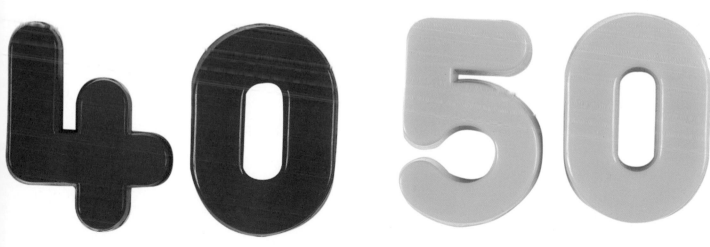

Forty

Fifty

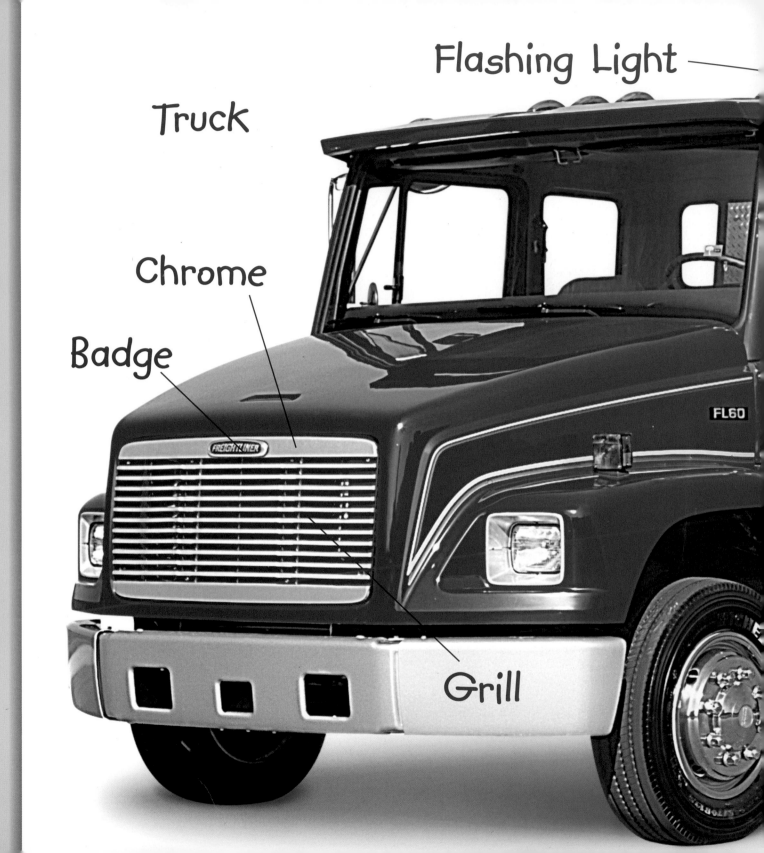

TOW-TRUCK

Flashing Light

Truck

Chrome

Badge

Grill

FL60

FREIGHTLINER

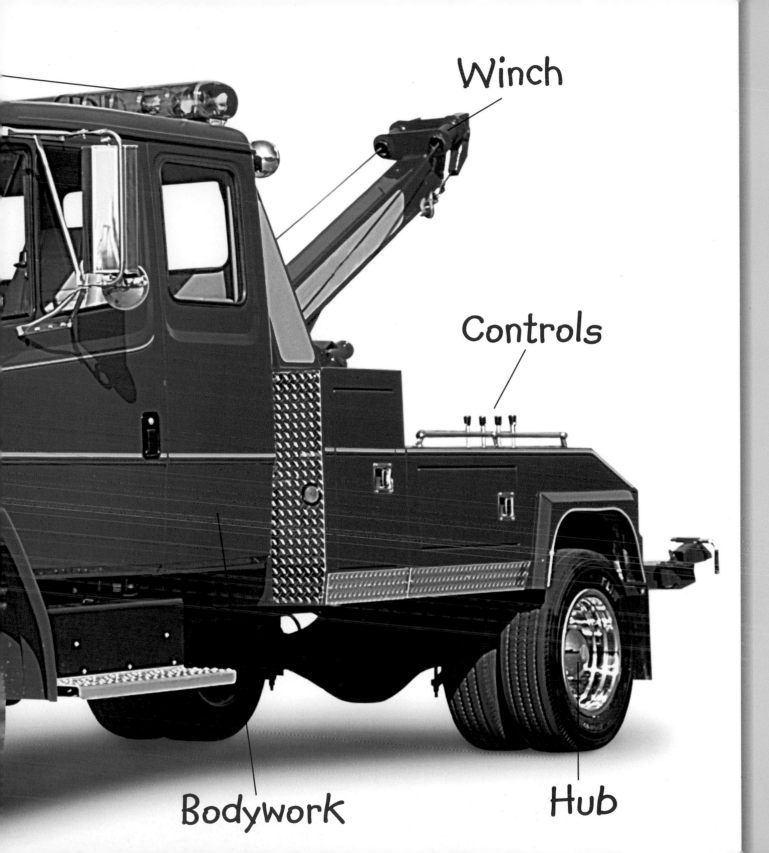

Winch

Controls

Bodywork

Hub

Chickpeas

Dishwasher Tablets

Beads

Dominoes

Zip

Fire Lighters

Marbles

Pine Cones

DOG

Muzzle

Paw

Claw

Pad

Flank

Tail

Fur

227

Puppy

Circle

Heart

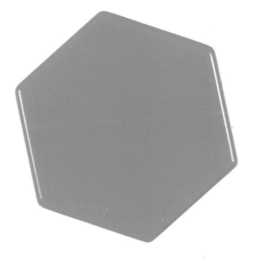

Polygon

Square

Oval

Rectangle

Star

Triangle

229

AEROPLANE

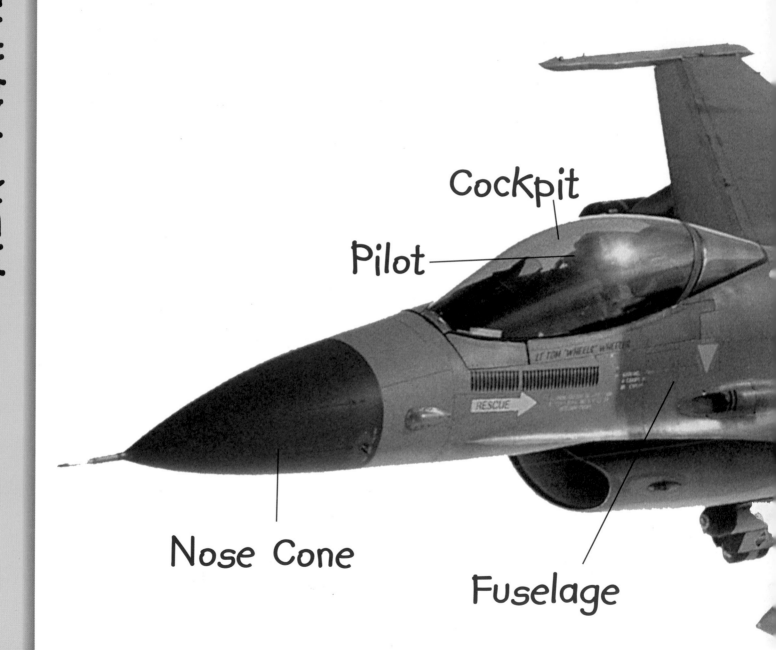

Cockpit

Pilot

Nose Cone

Fuselage

Wing

Undercarriage

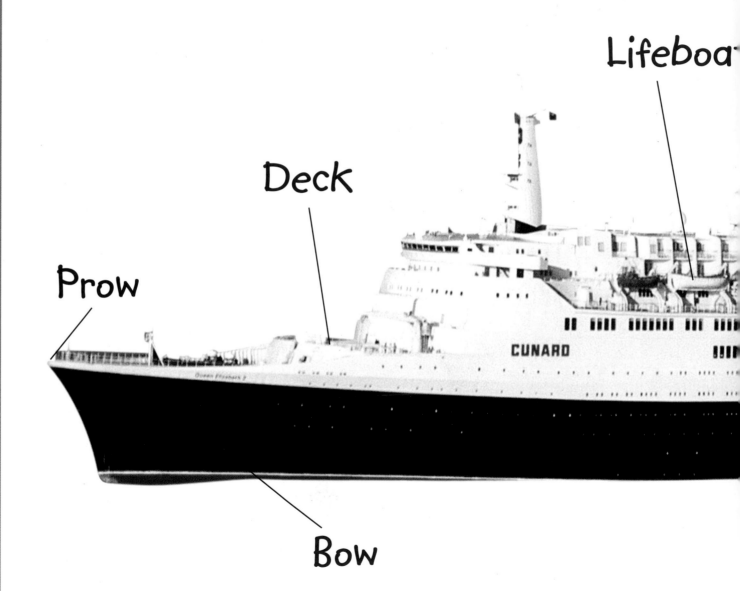

Lifeboat

Deck

Prow

Bow

CUNARD

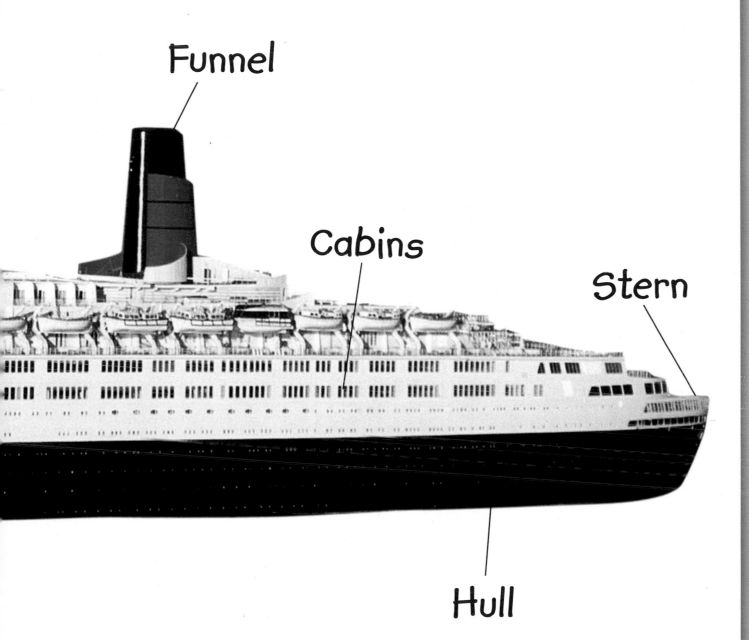

Funnel

Cabins

Stern

Hull

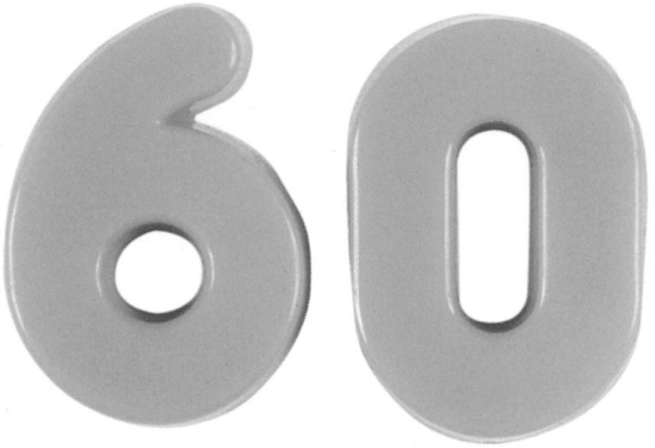

60

Sixty

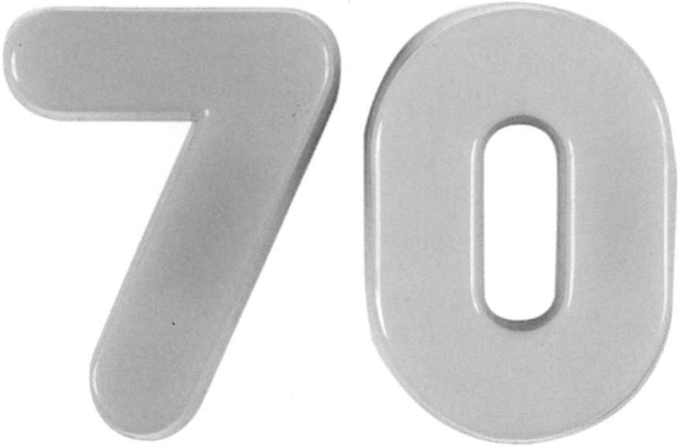

70

Seventy

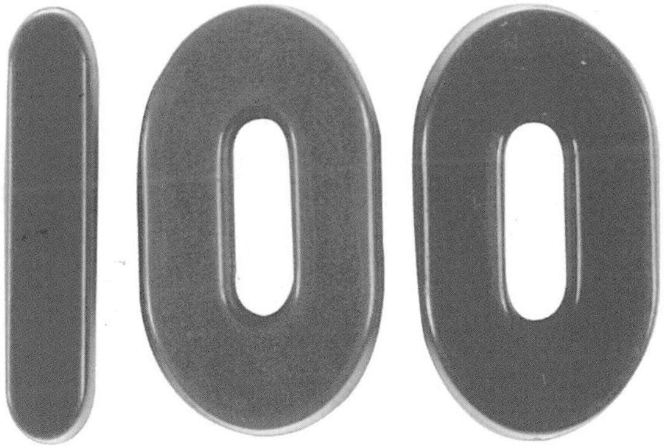

100

One Hundred

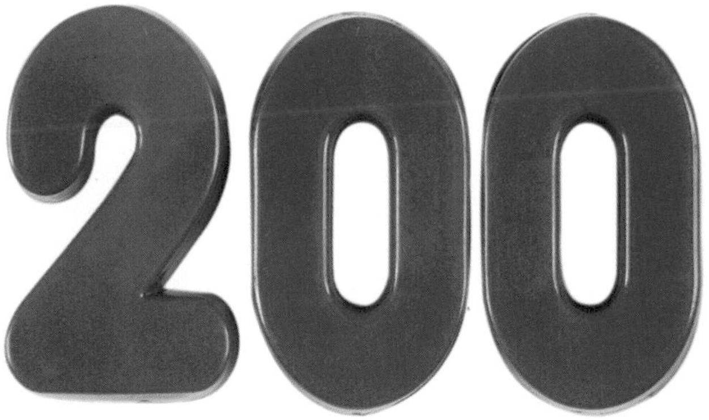

200

Two Hundred

Eighty

Ninety

Three Hundred

Four Hundred

235

Add

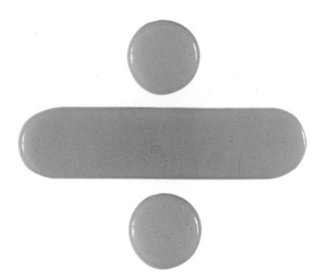

Divide

Percent

Full Stop

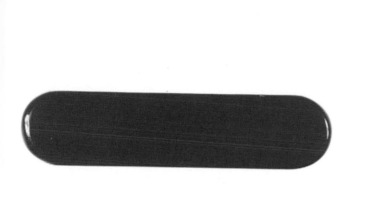

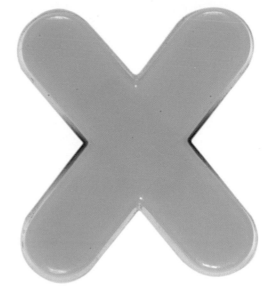

Subtract

Multiply

Comma

Equals

500 **Five Hundred**

600 **Six Hundred**

900 **Nine Hundred**

700 800

Seven Hundred · · · · · · Eight Hundred

1000

One Thousand

INDEX

A

add. 237
address book. 175
alligator. 81
almonds. 179
anti-perspirant 83
ankle. 197
anorak 141
antelope. 183
apple 49
apron 65
arch 197
arm. 199
arm chair 105
aubergine. 125
aviary 209
avocado 125
avocado 125

B

back 187
back brush. 7
badge 223
badminton racket 181
bag 77
bails 109
banana 49
bandage 73
banknotes 31

bark. 29
barn 213
barometer 169
barrier 207
basket. 71
bass guitar 145
bath. 3
bathmat 7
bay 191
beach 97
beach towel 5
beads 225
beam 215
beaters. 65
beetle 61
bellows 39
belt 139
berries 217
bib 37
big toe 197
binoculars 165
bird feeder 51
birdbath 51
birdseed 51
biscuits. 85
black. 15
blackberries 49
blade 119
blanket 93
bleach 13
blind. 161
bloom 185
blouse. 75
blue. 15
board game. 147

boat 123
bodywork 223
bollard 203
bolt 115
bone 95
bonnet 187
book 31
book shelves 169
boot 187
boots 19
bottle banks 203
bouncer 215
bouncy castle 45
bouncy slide 45
bow 233
boxfile 33
boxer shorts 27
bracelet 79
brake cables 193
brake-light 187
brakes 193
brazil nuts 179
bread board 67
bread knife 67
bricklayer's trowel 115
bricks 113
briefcase 89
broccoli 125
broom 55
brown 17
brush 13
bucket 11
bud 185
building blocks 147
bull 201

bumper 187
burgundy 17
bus shelter 203
bush 29
butcher's shop 203
butter 63
button 103

C

cabins 233
cable 43
calculator 33
calf 199
camera 31
camera case 31
canada goose 217
candle 105
candlestick 105
cap 139
car garage 205
car keys 175
car roof 187
car showroom 205
car sponge 11
car wing 189
card 163
car jack 155
carpet 143
carpet shampooer 137
carriages 123
carrot 85
carton 57
cash bag 99
casserole dish 69

INDEX

castors. 101
cat food 63
caterpillars 59
cat's bed. 169
cauliflower 125
cd rack 165
centipedes 59
cereal. 9
chain 3
chair 105
change. . . . . : . 175
cheek 195
cheese 57
cheetah 61
cherries 49
chest. 199
chickpeas 225
chimney 191
chimpanzee 61
chin 195
chisel 119
chocolate bar. 179
chocolate biscuits. 179
chrome 223
chutney. 57
circle. 229
city. 207
clamp. 119
clarinet 91
classical guitar. 91
claw 227
cleaner 13
clementine. 47
cliffs. 97
climbing frame. 215

cling film 149
clip 101
clock 105
cloth 11
cloud 131
clove 125
coach. 123
coal 39
coat hanger 27
cockpit. 231
coffee beans 159
coffee table. 169
coins 31
colander 69
collar 27
coloured pencils 101
colouring book 147
comma 237
compact disc 107
compass 19
computer 93
concrete. 143
controls. 223
cooker 23
cool box 5
copse 209
corduroy shirt 139
cork 21
corkscrew. 65
cotton reel 103
cotton wool 73
countryside 97
credit card 89
cricket ball 109
cricket bat 109

cricket gloves. 109
cricket pads 109
crisps 149
crowbar 115
cup 169
curtain 93
cushion 105
cuticle 197
cutlery. 21
cutters. 117
cuttlefish 5
cycle helmet 181
cycling 215

D

daisy. 19
deck 233
decorator 35
deer 183
desert 97
detergent. 11
dice. 147
digger. 43
disc. 193
dish cloth. 127
dishwasher tablets. 225
dispenser 99
divide 237
document case. 33
dog. 95
dog biscuits 95
dog brush. 95
dog bed 95
dog bowl 95

dog collar 95
dolphin. 183
dominoes. 225
door 189
doorbell. 41
door chain 41
door knocker 41
doormat 41
dove 177
drain 173
drawings. 151
dress 75
dressing 73
dressing gown. 135
dried apricots. 49
drill 117
drill bits 115
drink. 21
drinking bottle 167
driver 43
driveway. 191
drum. 91
duck 177
dumper truck. 123
dunes 97
duster 13
dustpan 13
duvet 135
duvet cover. 135

E

eagle 171
ear 195
earrings 79

INDEX

earth 143
eggcup 9
eggs 57
eight 219
eight hundred 239
eighteen 221
eighty 235
elbow 199
electric guitar 91
elephant 61
eleven 219
emu 213
engine 193
engine oil 155
envelope 175
equals 237
exercise book 167
exhaust 187
extension lead 25
eye 195
eyebrow 195
eyelash 195

F

fabric conditioner 71
face mask 157
fan 161
feather 87
felt tip pens 151
fence 53
ferris wheel 45
field 29
fifteen 219
fifty 221

film 31
finger 197
fir tree 209
fire 39
fire lighters 225
fireplace 39
fire tongs 39
first aid kit 155
fish 81
fish and chip shop 205
five 211
five hundred 239
flag 207
flag pole 207
flamingo 183
flank 227
flannel 83
flash cards 161
flashing light 223
flats 205
fleece 139
flip-flops 153
float 43
flock 217
flood 131
floorboards 143
floss 83
flower 185
flower pot 53
flowers 29
fly 59
fly swat 129
foil 149
folder 167
fondants 179

football III
foot pump 155
forehead 195
fork 37
forks 193
forty 221
fountain 209
fountain pen 89
four 211
four hundred 235
fourteen 219
frame 105
fridge magnets 69
fridge and freezer 23
fried egg 159
frog 81
front 187
front door 191
frying-pan 67
full stop 237
fungus 177
funnel 65, 233
fur 227
fuselage 231

G

gable 191
garage 173
garden 51
garden fork 55
garden gate 177
garden tap 25
garlic 125
gerbera 185

ginger root 159
giraffes 61
glass 21
glasses 79
globe 147
goat 201
goblet 169
goggles 153
golf ball III
goose 201
gorilla 81
grapes 49
grass 53
grate 39
grater 67
green 15
greenhouse 51
grey 15
grill 223
gutter 113

H

hacksaw 119
hair 195
hair brush 79
hair dryer 77
ham roll 149
hammer 117
hand fork 55
hand cream 77
handle 189
hang-glider 213
hazelnuts 179
head 199

INDEX

headlight 187
headphones 107
headscarf 141
heart 229
hedge 53
heel 197
helter-skelter 45
hen 201
hi-fi 107
high-heeled shoes 75
hip 199
hippopotamus 183
hoe 25
holdall 181
hole punch 99
hooks 115
horses 201
hose 25
hot air balloon 213
hot water bottle 135
house keys 89
hub 223
hub cap 189
hull 233

I

ice cream cone 179
icicles 177
index finger 197
indicator 187
ink 89
instant coffee 63
instructions 33
iron 71

ironing board 71
island 209

J

jam 9
jar 57
jeans 139
jewellery box 79
jigsaw puzzle 121
joggers 153
joint 197
jug 69
juice 57
jump leads 155
jumper 27
jungle 133

K

kerb 113
kettle 23
keyboard 99
key-fob 175
keyhole 41
kidney beans 159
kingfisher 171
kit bag 153
kitchen paper 137
kiwi fruit 49
knee 199
knife 37
knitting needles 103
knuckle 197

L

laces 19
ladder 43
ladle 69
lake 97
lamp post 113
laundry 71
lawnmower 25
lead 95
leaf 185
leaves 53
leg 199
lemon squeezer 69
lemon 17
lemons 47
lemur 183
lentils 85
letter 175
letterbox 41
lid 101
lifeboat 233
light 169
light blue 17
light bulb 129
lightning 131
lily 185
lime 49
lino 143
lion 61
lips 195
lipstick 79
litter bin 177
lizard 81
loaf 21
logs 39
lollipops 163
lorry 123
lotion 79
loudspeaker 107

M

magazine 31
make-up bag 77
mallet 119
mango 47
manhole cover 173
map 19
marbles 225
marker pen 101
mascot 121
masking tape 157
mat 129
match box 63
matches 63
medicine 73
melon 47
metal file 117
microphone 145
microscope 93
microwave 23
milk 9
mirror 77
mixer 65
mobile 163
mobile phone 89
model train 121
money box 93
monitor 99

INDEX

monkey 183
mop. 137
mosquito 59
moth. 59
mountains 97
mouse. 93
mouth 195
mudguard. 193
muesli 9
mug 93
mules 75
multiply. 237
mushroom 125
musical notes 145
music-stand 145
mustard. 159
muzzle. 227

N

nail 197
nail file. 75
nail brush. 7
nails 43
neck 195
necklace 79
needle 103
net. 87
nettles 29
nine. 219
nine hundred 239
nineteen 221
ninety 235
nose 195
nose cone. 231

nostril 195
notepad. 33
nozzle 25
number plate. 187
nut. 115

O

obelisk 209
ochre 17
oil 157
oil lamp 129
oil-rig 213
ointment 73
olives. 21
one. 211
one hundred. 235
one thousand 239
onion 125
orange. 15
orange juice 9
oval. 229
owl. 171

P

pac-a-mac 141
packed lunch 167
pad. 227
padlock. 43
paint. 35
paint brushes 35
paint roller 35
paint box 151
painting 169

palm 197
palm tree 217
pane 41
panel saw 117
paperclips 99
park bench 177
parking bay 173
parking meter 203
parquet 143
parrot 171
parsley 57
parsnip 85
passport 33
pasta 69
path 19
patio 51
paving-stone 173
paw 227
peaches 47
peacock 81
peak 139
peanuts 179
peapods 85
pear 47
peas 85
pebbles 5
peeler 65
pegs 71
pelican crossing 203
pelicans 171
pen 217
pencil sharpener 99
pencil-case 167
penknife 31
pepper mill 37

percent 237
perfume 77
petrol cap 189
petrol tank 193
piano 145
piano stool 145
picnic hamper 87
picture 105
pillar 51
pillow 135
pillowcase 135
pilot 231
pine cones 225
pine nut kernels 159
pineapple 47
pink 17
pins 103
pipe 157
place mat 21
plant 185
plaque 41
plaster 73
plate 127
playdough 161
playing cards 161
pliers 119
plug 3
plug hole 3
poker 39
polish 11
polyanthus 133
polygon 229
poppy 185
porch 191
poster paints 151

INDEX

pot plant 105
praying mantis 59
present 163
printer 101
protractor 167
prow 233
pruning saw 53
public house 205
public toilet 203
puddle 141
pullover 165
puppet 163
puppy 227
purple 17
purse 175
pushchair 163
putty knife 115, 157
pylon 207
pyrex bowl 69

R

rabbit 201
radar dish 213
radiator 187
radio 101
rag 11
rail 93
railing 205
railway track 147
rain 141
rainbow 131
raindrops 141
rain hat 19
rake 55

ram 201
razor 83
receipt 175
recorder 91
rectangle 229
red 15
red pepper 125
remote control 107
reversing light 187
rhinoceros 61
ribbon 103
rice 85
ring 77
road atlas 155
road signs 113
robot 165
rocket 161
rollerblading 215
rolling pin 67
roof 191
rope 87
rose 185
roundabout 45
rubber 151
rubber bands 99
rubber duck 7
rubber gloves 127
rug 143
ruler 167
rushes 209

S

safety goggles 157
safety pins 73

salad 85
salt-cellar 37
sand 87
sandpaper 157
sandwich 149
sandwich box 149
satchel 167
satellite dish 173
sauce 37
saucepan 67
saucer 169
scaffolding 205
scales 67
scarf 139
scissors 157
scoop 65
scorpion 59
scourer 127
scrambled eggs 21
scraper 35
screen 107
screwdriver 117
screws 129
scrubbing brush 13
seagull 171
seat 193
seaweed 5
secateurs 55
seedlings 53
seed tray 53
see-saw 215
serviette 37
set square 115
seven 211
seven hundred 239

seventeen 221
seventy 235
shaving-brush 83
shears 55
sheep 201
sheet 135
sheet music 145
shells 5
shin 199
shirt 27
shopping list 175
shore 97
shoulders 199
shuttlecock 181
side 189
side window 189
sieve 67
signpost 173
sink 23
six 211
six hundred 239
sixteen 221
sixty 235
skateboard 181
skirt 75
sky 29
skyscrapers 213
sleeves 27
slide 215
slippers 75
sloes 133
snail 59
snake 81
snakes and ladders 121
snow 131

INDEX

soap 7
soapsuds 127
soap tray 7
soapy water 11
socks 27
soft toy 163
sole 197
space shuttle 121
spade 55
spaghetti 63
spanner 117
spider's web 217
spinner 45
spirit-level 35
sponge 7
spoon 37
spray 13
spring onions 85
square 229
squash ball 111
squash racket 111
squeegee 11
stain remover 137
stalk 47, 185
stamps 101
stapler 33
staples 33
star 229
starfish 5
statue 177
steam train 123
stem 185
step-ladder 35
stern 233
sticky tack 101

stile 19
stone 125
stool 23
stopper 135
storm 131
strainer 65
strap 89
strawberry 47
straws 63
stream 19
string 129
stumps 109
subtract 237
succulent 133
suit jacket 139
sundial 51
sunglasses 31
sun hat 5
sunscreen 87
sunset 131
sunshade 87
suspension 193
suspension bridge 207
swan 217
sweatshirt 27
sweeping brush 137
sweets 149
swimming cap 153
swimming trunks 153
swimsuit 153
swing 215
swivel chair 101
synthesiser 91